Learning Objectives For:

TEAM BUILDING

The objectives for *Team Building, Fourth Edition* are listed below. They have been developed to guide you, the reader, to the core issues covered in this book.

THE OBJECTIVES OF THIS BOOK ARE:

❏ 1) To spell out the differences between a group and a team

❏ 2) To present tips for becoming an effective team leader

❏ 3) To explore behavior styles and the strengths each style brings to the team

❏ 4) To demonstrate ways to promote open communication and team involvement

❏ 5) To explain the importance of helping team members to achieve and grow in their jobs

ASSESSING YOUR PROGRESS

In addition to the learning objectives, Crisp Learning has developed an **assessment** that covers the fundamental information presented in this book. A 25-item, multiple-choice and true-false questionnaire allows the reader to evaluate his or her comprehension of the subject matter. To buy the assessment and answer key, go to www.crisplearning.com and search on the book title, or call 1-800-442-7477.

Assessments should not be used in any employee selection process.

About the Authors

This fourth edition of *Team Building* was authored by Barb Wingfield, who is uniquely qualified to carry on the legacy of two favorite Crisp authors, Elwood Chapman and Robert Maddux. Through her update of *Winning at Human Relations,* a perennial bestseller by "Chap" and now this update of Maddux's *Team Building,* Barb once again demonstrates her talent for helping people understand and improve how they interact with others.

Barb Wingfield is founder of Morale Builders and works with organizations that want to cultivate great employees. She presents keynotes and seminars and consults with organizations throughout the United States. She is member of the National Speakers Association and the National Association for Employee Recognition. She is the author of *Reasons to Say WOW!!! A Celebration of Life's Simple Pleasures* and co-author of another Crisp book, *Retaining Your Employees.*

She is eager to hear your stories about team building. You can reach her at barb@moralebuilders.com or visit her Web site at www.moralebuilders.com.

In Memoriam

The late Robert Maddux was an extraordinary individual. For more than 30 years, he designed and delivered management-skills seminars throughout the world, helping large corporations and small businesses improve their productivity. Bob also authored several best-selling management books including *Effective Performance Appraisals, Delegating for Results, Building Teams for Your Small Business, Job Performance and Chemical Dependency, Successful Negotiation, Quality Interviewing,* and *Ethics in Business. Team Building* was his best-selling title, and this revision is based on the concepts Bob originally developed.

More than a million copies of Bob's books have been sold. They have served as the basis for several training videos and have been translated into more than 20 languages. Bob's genius of making complex things simple has helped untold numbers of readers worldwide become better managers. Bob was a true "people person" and his good nature and contributions to management are greatly missed, but live on through his published works.

Preface

Teams are everywhere we look. From our work environment to the volunteer work we do to our leisure time, teams play a role in our lives. Some teams are formally organized and some are loosely bound together, but they are all trying to achieve a goal. It would be wonderful if we could observe team structures and pinpoint one element that makes a team successful, but as in so many situations it is a variety of things.

This book addresses many of the components needed to build a successful team—planning, organizing, commitment, vision, and so on. The sound principles that Robert Maddux wrote about are still applicable today. It was an honor to revise this book and update the examples and work situations.

To help you, the reader, better understand these concepts, I have selected the analogy of building a house to illustrate building a team. Whether or not you have ever built a house, been involved in a remodeling project, or watched a building project unfold, I believe that you will be able to identify with the core elements needed to build a team—and a house.

As you read this book, look for the similarities between your work environment and the concepts described. Select the ideas and concepts that will help your team grow and achieve new goals. Enjoy the building process!

Barb Wingfield

Barb Wingfield

Acknowledgments

I would like to thank my team of cheerleaders who keep me centered and on task both personally and professionally: Bob, Brian, Erin, Brad, Rebecca, Adam, Shirley, and Julie. A special thanks to Mike Foti, president of Leadership Builders; Christine Zust, president of Zust and Company; and Loran Zwerin from Zwerin and Associates, who offered their expertise. Thanks to Debbie Woodbury for her insight and help to make this revision the best possible for the readers. A special tip of the hat to the all the wonderful employees at Crisp who have worked to make this project great.

Contents

Part 4: Installing Windows to Better Communication

Part 5: Erecting a Stable Roof of Trust

Summary

Designing a Successful Blueprint for Your Team

The Purpose of a Blueprint

Before a blueprint for your new house can be drawn up, you must plan and discuss with the builder the features and characteristics you would like to include in the house. The blueprint is then designed to reflect your taste and include the features that will make your house functional.

The blueprint serves as a guide for the builder to construct the house according to the plan you have agreed on. It also helps the builder determine the type and amount of materials needed. And the blueprint helps define what tradespeople will be needed on the team to build the house.

Organizing and planning for a great team is much like this process. Once you have determined in what ways a team would be helpful in your work environment, you can begin to assemble the team, just as contractors bring together their tradespeople. Take the time to draw up your "blueprint" and develop your guidebook for the team.

This is what this part is about: taking the time up front to define the qualities you need in the team and in your leadership style to help you achieve greater success through teamwork.

Distinguishing Teams from Groups

From the beginning, people have formed groups. Groups provide the basis for family living, protection, warfare, government, recreation, and work. Group behavior has ranged from chaos to dramatic success, but it is increasingly evident that groups enjoy their greatest success when they become more productive units called teams.

Managers in many organizations seem content with group performance. This is often because they have not thought beyond what is being accomplished to what might be achieved under slightly different circumstances. Other leaders using the same number of people doing similar tasks with the same technology somehow manage to improve productivity and profit dramatically by establishing a climate where people are willing to give their best and work together in teams.

Different Styles to Lead Each Unit

Uniting groups of people into teams, whether to solve a company shipping problem or to build a house, takes planning and effort. Team leaders exhibit different styles than those who are content managing a group. Individuals' life experiences and the values they have adopted over the years shape these styles.

Given today's rapid rate of organizational change and the changing needs of people, it is important for those "in charge" to reevaluate and modify their styles regularly. This is the only way you can make the adaptations necessary to continue to be effective.

The charts on the following pages will help you to see the differences between groups and teams and the different characteristics required to lead each unit. Plan to make any needed changes in your style and evaluate the results carefully. Keep making adjustments until you achieve the results you desire. And with the characteristics of team-centered leadership in mind, make a commitment to creating and supporting a team effort. Stay on the alert for additional ways to improve your leadership.

Building Tip —————————————

"There are no problems we cannot solve together and very few that we can solve by ourselves."

—**U.S. President Lyndon Johnson**

Defining Group vs. Team Characteristics

To help you determine whether you are working with a group or a team, compare the characteristics in the two columns. In which category is your current unit?

Groups	Teams
Members think they are grouped together for administrative purposes only. Individuals work independently, sometimes at cross-purposes with others.	Members recognize their interdependence and understand that personal and team goals are best accomplished with mutual support. Time is not wasted struggling over "turf" or attempting personal gain at others' expense.
Members tend to focus on themselves because they are not sufficiently involved in planning the unit's objectives. Their approach to their job is simply that of a hired hand.	Members feel a sense of ownership for their jobs and the unit because they are committed to goals they helped establish.
Members are told what to do rather than being asked what the best approach would be. Suggestions are not encouraged.	Members contribute to the organization's success by applying their unique talent and knowledge to team objectives.
Members distrust their colleagues' motives because they do not understand the others' role. Expressions of opinion or disagreement are considered divisive or non-supportive.	Members work in a climate of trust and are encouraged to openly express ideas, opinions, disagreements, and feelings. Questions are welcomed.
Members are so cautious about what they say that real understanding is not possible. Game playing may occur and communications traps may be set to catch the unwary.	Members practice open and honest communication. They make an effort to understand one another's point of view.

CONTINUED

Groups (cont'd)	Teams (cont'd)
Members may receive good training but are limited by the supervisor or other group members in applying their training to the job.	Members are encouraged to develop skills and apply what they learn on the job. They receive the support of the team.
Members find themselves in conflict that they do not know how to resolve. Their supervisor may put off intervention until serious damage is done.	Members recognize conflict is normal in human interaction but they view such situations as an opportunity for new ideas and creativity. They work to resolve conflict quickly and constructively.
Members may or may not participate in decisions affecting the team. Conformity often appears more important than positive results.	Members participate in decisions affecting the team but understand that their leader must make a final ruling whenever the team cannot decide or in an emergency. Positive results, not conformity, are the goal.

Group-Centered Managers vs. Team-Centered Leaders

See how team-centered leadership differs from group-centered management and think about which qualities best describe you at this time.

Group-Centered	Team-Centered
Overriding concern to meet current goals inhibits thought about what might be accomplished through reorganizing to enhance member contributions.	Current goals are taken in stride. Can be a visionary about what the people can achieve as a team. Can share vision and act accordingly.
Reactive to upper management, peers, and employees. Finds it easier to go along with the crowd.	Proactive in most relationships. Exhibits personal style. Can stimulate excitement and action. Inspires teamwork and mutual support.
Willing to involve people in planning and problem solving to some extent, but within limits.	Can get people involved and committed. Makes it easy for others to see opportunities for teamwork. Allows people to perform.
Resents or distrusts employees who know their jobs better than the manager.	Looks for people who want to excel and can work constructively with others. Feels role is to encourage and facilitate this behavior.
Sees group problem solving as a waste of time or an abdication of managerial responsibility.	Considers problem solving the responsibility of team members.
Controls information and communicates only what group members need or want to know.	Communicates fully and openly. Welcomes questions. Allows the team to do its own filtering.
Ignores conflict between staff members or with other groups.	Mediates conflict before it becomes destructive.

CONTINUED

Group-Centered (cont'd)	Team-Centered (cont'd)
Sometimes slow to recognize individual or group achievements.	Makes an effort to see that both individual and team accomplishments are recognized at the right time in an appropriate manner.
Sometimes modifies group agreements to suit personal convenience.	Keeps commitments and expects the same in return.

Increasing Productivity Through Teamwork

There are groups of many different types with extremely varied purposes and goals. Whether these groups are organized to perform business, community, and governmental functions, all groups can achieve far more when they work as teams.

When productive teams are compared with less productive groups, important differences involving the application of team concepts come into view. Here is an example:

> A study was made of 20 coal mines operating in the same geologic structure, drawing from the same labor pool, and subject to the same governmental regulations. Productivity was measured in tons of coal produced per employee per shift.
>
> The mine with the highest productivity delivered 242 tons per employee contrasted with the lowest, which mined 58 tons per employee. The other mines were somewhere in between.

Conclusions from this study were summarized as follows: "The primary difference was the way in which company management worked with the employees. The most productive mine provided employees with significantly more individual responsibility and involvement in goal setting and problem solving."

Teamwork at All Levels

As can be seen in the mining example, effective teamwork knows no level. It is just as important among top executives as it is among middle managers, first-line supervisors, or front-line employees. The absence of teamwork at any level (or between levels) will limit organizational effectiveness and can eventually kill an organization.

If you are waiting for someone in higher management to tell you to build a team, you may be limiting the success of your unit and yourself. Thinking, proactive managers do not wait for a directive from above. Instead, they begin immediately to develop solid management skills. If teamwork is lacking, good managers can identify where the problems are and initiate corrective action to change things until the desired results are achieved.

Within effective teams, individual members play an assigned role using their individual talents to the best advantage. Looking again at the house-building example, few people have all the skills to construct the foundation, lay the bricks for the fireplace, and finish the drywall. But when each tradesperson on the team completes his assigned tasks, the objectives are usually achieved and the house is completed.

Groups develop and transform into teams when all members understand their common purpose. On the other hand, when group members work as individuals, they usually fail. The key to success is being willing to plan, work, and reevaluate as the progress unfolds.

Building Tip

"When teamwork works well, you feel a deep level of connection to team members. The energy you receive from the experience builds an unstoppable momentum that makes you feel that anything is possible and achievable."

–Christine Zust

The Benefits of Team Building

If a leader does not place a high value on teamwork, it will not occur. But leaders sometimes assign a low priority to team building because they have not considered the advantages that can accrue from a well-executed team effort. Teamwork takes conscious effort to develop and continuous effort to maintain. But well-executed team efforts can result in big rewards, as listed below. Check (✔) those you would like to achieve with your teams.

- ❑ The team and individual members can set realistic, achievable goals because those responsible for doing the work contribute to setting the goals.

- ❑ Employees and leaders commit to support one another.

- ❑ Communication is open. The expression of new ideas, improved work methods, and problems and concerns is encouraged.

- ❑ Problem solving is more effective because the team's expertise is available.

- ❑ Performance feedback is more meaningful because team members understand what is expected and can monitor their performance against expectations.

- ❑ Conflict is understood as normal and viewed as an opportunity to solve problems. Through open discussion it can be resolved before it becomes destructive.

- ❑ Balance is maintained between group productivity and the satisfaction of personal team members' needs.

- ❑ The team is recognized for outstanding results, as are individuals for their personal contributions.

- ❑ Members are encouraged to test their abilities and try out ideas, which stimulates individuals to become stronger performers.

- ❑ Team members recognize the important of disciplined work habits and conform their behavior to meet team standards.

- ❑ Learning to work effectively as a team in one unit is good preparation for working as a team with other units. It is also good preparation for advancement.

Building Tip

Teamwork and productivity go hand in hand.

DOES YOUR ATTITUDE SUPPORT TEAM BUILDING?

When team building is understood and applied at all organizational levels, transforming groups into teams throughout the organization becomes much easier. A positive attitude toward team building is essential. The following attitudes support team building and will help you identify your strengths and determine areas for improvement. Circle the number that best reflects where you fall on the scale. The higher the number, the more the characteristic describes you. When you have finished, total the numbers circled and note this total in the space provided.

1. When I select employees, I choose those who can meet the job requirements and work well with others.   7 6 5 4 3 2 1

2. I give employees a sense of ownership by involving them in goal setting, problem solving, and productivity improvement.   7 6 5 4 3 2 1

3. I provide team spirit by encouraging people to work together and to support one another on related activities.   7 6 5 4 3 2 1

4. I talk with people openly and honestly and encourage the same communication in return.   7 6 5 4 3 2 1

5. I keep agreements with my team members because their trust is essential to my leadership.   7 6 5 4 3 2 1

6. I help team members get to know one another so they can learn to trust, respect, and appreciate individual talent and ability.   7 6 5 4 3 2 1

7. I ensure employees have the required training to do their job and know how it is to be applied.   7 6 5 4 3 2 1

8. I understand that conflict within groups in normal, but I work to resolve it quickly and fairly before it can become destructive.   7 6 5 4 3 2 1

9. I believe people will perform as a team when they know what is expected and what benefits will accrue.   7 6 5 4 3 2 1

10. I am willing to replace members who cannot or will not meet reasonable standards after appropriate coaching.   7 6 5 4 3 2 1

TOTAL_____

A score between 60 and 70 indicates a positive attitude toward people—the attitude needed to build and maintain a strong team. A score between 40 and 59 is acceptable, and with reasonable effort, team building should be possible for you. If you scored below 40, you must carefully examine your attitude in light of current management philosophy.

Building Tip

Approach people with respect—approach tasks with a can-do attitude.

CASE STUDY: CAN THIS SUPERVISOR BE SAVED?

Mary Lou has been supervisor to five employees for about three months. It is her first supervisory assignment, and she has had little training.

Although each employee has a different job with its own standards, the tasks are interrelated and the success of the unit depends on a cooperative effort. May Lou has worked hard to assign tasks, set deadlines, and solve problems to achieve the desired results. The poor skills of two employees and the constant bickering within the group, however, have caused delays and frustration for everyone. Mary Lou would like to spend more time with her employees but paperwork and reporting seem to consume most of her time. She also has recently begun to stay in her office more because of the hostility among the employees. Group productivity has fallen below expectations, and Mary Lou is increasingly afraid she might be fired.

What might Mary Lou do to save her job and turn the performance of the unit around?

_____

_____

_____

_____

_____

_____

_____

Compare your answer with the authors' response in the back of the book.

Building a Strong Foundation

The Importance of a Strong Foundation

A strong foundation is essential in building a sturdy house that will stand the test of time. The foundation's purpose is to support all other parts of the house so they will function correctly. If a poor foundation is built and the house begins to sag on one corner, the doors might not open correctly.

A successful team also must build a strong foundation. If your team's foundation is weak in one area, you risk the chance of poor results in that area and the others it might affect.

When building a house, the foundation design depends on your budget, location, building requirements, and your personal taste. The same holds true when you are building a foundation for your team. A foundation for a team working to improve delivery service of its products is different from a team working together every day for greater productivity and efficiency. Indeed, no matter what your situation and goals are, building a strong foundation is essential to achieving your goals.

The future, longevity, and sturdiness of your team rest on the foundation you build. Your leadership skills will be put to use and challenged as you strive to build a strong foundation. This part will help you determine how much work you must do to become an effective team leader.

Taking the Time to Plan

Teams need to know why they exist, what they are supposed to accomplish, and who else is involved. If these areas are fuzzy, frustration results. Team members expect their leader to know the direction they are to take and how they are to coordinate with other groups to reach their goals. To accomplish this requires effective planning.

Planning is the thinking that precedes the work. If planning is not done, time and effort is usually wasted. If you fail to plan for the correct materials and people to build your foundation, you risk having a faulty foundation. Take the time to plan.

Effective planning includes the following elements. Check (✔) your proficiency level for each.

Do Well	Should Improve	
❑	❑	1. Interpreting goals passed down as the result of planning at higher levels.
❑	❑	2. Articulating organizational needs (including those of the team) into team goals and objectives.
❑	❑	3. Formulating implementation plans by examining alternatives and selecting activities that lead to successful results.
❑	❑	4. Identifying resources needed to achieve goals (people, time, money, materials, and facilities) and ensuring they are available.
❑	❑	5. Establishing time lines and completion target dates.
❑	❑	6. Determining standards of performance and how results will be measured.

Building Tip

Employees can make important contributions to planning once they become committed to the process. If you plan well, your team leadership will be much more effective. If you need to improve, do it now.

Using Organizational Skills

Once planning is underway, organization becomes important. Resources—people, capital, raw materials, and technology—must be coordinated effectively to achieve team goals. One of the strengths of a good leader is the ability to see a future for the organization that is better than what currently exists. This view must then be communicated in such a way that employees can organize their resources to achieve the desired results in an inspiring way.

Team members look to the leader for direction and the allocation of resources. Leaders must be organized and capable of helping the team organize itself to accomplish goals. If organization is poor, the group will become confused, discouraged, and argumentative. Teamwork will be impossible.

Key aspects of organization are listed below. Check (✔) your proficiency in each.

Do Well	Should Improve	
❑	❑	1. I can divide work into logical tasks and groupings.
❑	❑	2. I know how to secure the resources required to achieve goals.
❑	❑	3. I am comfortable assigning tasks, resources, and responsibilities to team members based on functions and skills.
❑	❑	4. I can establish guidelines to coordinate activities between team members and other groups involved with the outcome.
❑	❑	5. I design information systems that assure appropriate feedback as the work progresses.
❑	❑	6. I can establish communications networks to ensure there is a free flow of information up, down, and across organizational lines.

Building Tip

Employees can make important contributions to the organizing process from their knowledge and experience. Employee involvement can enhance teamwork and efficiency. The better your organizational skills, the stronger you should be as a leader. If you need to improve, do it now.

Building a Climate for Motivation

Successful supervisors understand that individual employees are responsible for their own motivation. What the supervisor or employer is responsible for is working to create an atmosphere where employees feel appreciated and recognized for their contributions. Some supervisors have adopted the mind-set of "they get paid to work; why should I thank them!" But supervisors with this belief probably will not realize the full potential of their employees.

Open Communication

Most employees respond positively when you share with them the vision and goals of the team and the organization. People like to be kept "in the loop." Water-cooler or break-room gossip can slow productivity and undermine the work environment if people are spending their time speculating on changes in the organization.

Employees are more motivated to a quality performance if they feel they are part of the communication circle. A supervisor must be sensitive to recognizing these employee needs and must design ways to meet them while achieving the organization's goals.

Individual Motivations

Establishing yourself as a strong leader also requires creating a working climate in which team members can meet individual needs while achieving team goals. No single technique works for everyone because people work for a variety of reasons.

What is important for one person may have little significance to another. Some people work for basic survival needs while others are seeking security. Some work to fulfill ego satisfaction or something even deeper. Motivation is personal and supervisors must get to know individual employees to learn what motivates them. This requires time and effort but the results are worth it, as illustrated in the story on the next page.

Recognizing Individual Team Members

Mike was stymied. His team was finishing a major project that was ahead of schedule and a little under budget. Mike wanted to recognize the team members in his engineering department for their stellar contribution to the project, but he could not think of a gift that would be suitable for all members.

That evening he was sharing his dilemma with his wife Julie. She immediately asked, "Why do you have to get all the team members the same gift? I would never buy the same gift for all of our children." Mike sat there dazed for a moment—why hadn't he realized the importance of treating team members as individuals who contributed to the team? Mike and Julie started to work on gift ideas for each person.

Two weeks later Mike organized a group lunch for the team members to celebrate the project completion. He was so happy that he had a gift for each team member that reflected the individual's interest or hobby. The team members were thrilled with their personalized gifts. Mike learned a valuable lesson, that even though people function as a team it is important to recognize their individual strengths and uniqueness.

How Well Do You Motivate Others?

How good are you at building a climate that motivates employees to be successful? Check (✔) your proficiency in each of the following elements of effective employee motivation. When these elements are combined, both individual and team success is possible.

Do Well	Should Improve	
❑	❑	1. Ensuring each employee knows what is expected and how performance will be measured.
❑	❑	2. Getting to know employees as individuals to learn their needs.
❑	❑	3. Providing the training and supervisory assistance necessary for each employee to achieve mutually established objectives.
❑	❑	4. Providing the resources required to perform the job.
❑	❑	5. Guiding and encouraging personal growth for individual employees.
❑	❑	6. Recognizing and rewarding good performance and correcting, or eliminating, poor performance when it occurs.

Building Tip

Good leaders know how to build a motivating climate. If you need to improve, do it now.

Establishing Accountability

A supervisor or builder must continually check the progress of the job. As the action progresses, modifying and adjusting the plan may be necessary to keep the team focused and on target. This process is called accountability.

Once a project has begun, an accountability system is needed to make sure it will progress according to plan and the ultimate objective will be achieved. Accountability should be established during the planning process and be as simple as possible. When the accountability system is in place, the leader and the team can compare what is happening with what was expected. From the ongoing results, it may be necessary to revise the objective, modify the plan, reorganize, or take added motivational steps or other appropriate action.

Important aspects of accountability are listed below. Indicate your proficiency with each by checking (✔) the appropriate box.

Do Well	Should Improve	
❑	❑	1. Establish accountability elements as part of the project plan.
❑	❑	2. Set up time schedules and checkpoints to measure progress.
❑	❑	3. Encourage feedback from team members throughout the project.
❑	❑	4. Evaluate problems or deviations from plans and then construct a new action plan that is timely and appropriate.
❑	❑	5. Adjust objectives, plans, resources, or motivational factors as required to meet the organizational goals.
❑	❑	6. Communicate progress and plan changes to those who need to know.

Building Tip

In a team situation, employees should, by their involvement, be responsible for much of the accountability. If you need to improve your skills in this area, do it now.

CASE STUDY: WHICH SUPERVISOR WOULD YOU PREFER?

Morgana and Jeff have just been promoted to their first supervisory position. Both have had considerable experience as senior micro-technicians before the promotion. One day during lunch, Morgana and Jeff shared plans for making the transition from technician to supervisor.

Morgana volunteered that she plans to concentrate on defining the work that needs to be done and then provide her employees with precise goals and standards. Because of her experience and knowledge, she will also prepare a detailed performance plan for each employee. She believes this approach will ensure the goals are met while giving her the control she needs to get the job done.

Jeff responded by saying he had already secured his manager's agreement to take a supervisory skills course to ensure he understood the management process. In the meantime, however, Jeff plans to involve his group in day-to-day planning, organizing, and problem solving. Jeff is confident of his ability but believes every member of his staff is competent and can make important contributions to the group's effectiveness. He also feels that individuals need the satisfaction that comes from being involved in a project.

For which of these supervisors would you rather work?

_____

_____

_____

_____

Compare your answer with the authors' responses in the back of the book.

Constructing a
Solid Framework

26

Assembling Your Team

Now that you have developed your blueprint and built your foundation, you are ready to start the framing of your team, giving it shape and definition.

People are the most critical part of any organization's success. Good people help ensure profitability, productivity, growth, and long-term survival. The team simply cannot sustain without qualified people. As a team leader, you must guide these people in learning to work together.

The following elements are critical in employee selection and placement. Indicate how well you perform in these areas by checking the appropriate box.

Do Well	Should Improve	
❏	❏	1. I analyze job requirements thoroughly before beginning the selection process.
❏	❏	2. I always probe for objective evidence of an applicant's skills, knowledge, past successes and failures, dependability, and attitude toward work, co-workers, supervision, and customers.
❏	❏	3. I describe my idea of teamwork to applicants and ask them to assess how they would work under team conditions.
❏	❏	4. I make sure each applicant understands the job requirements and expected standards of performance.
❏	❏	5. I evaluate facts carefully and avoid making premature conclusions or stereotyping while making a selection decision.
❏	❏	6. People I hire are placed in positions where there is potential for success.

Building Tip

If the people you select to be on your team are not successful, you will not be successful. If you need to improve your selection and placement practices, do it now.

Combining Various Behavior Styles

Everyone sees the world differently. We are all shaped by our background, where and when we were born, who raised us, where we went to school, and how we spent (and spend) our free time. Our heredity and environment have made us who we are today.

When selecting team members, it is wise to tap into as many viewpoints as possible by bringing together people with varied backgrounds and experiences. And another way to vary your team is by choosing members with different behavior styles.

Behavior styles, or personality types, can be described in many ways, and personality assessment instruments can provide detailed feedback about a person's primary and supporting personality characteristics. But you need not test people or conduct a psychological interview to learn someone's personality type. Once you know what to look and listen for, you can learn to identify dominant type or style by simply paying attention to the person for a little while.

In her book *The Business of Listening**, author Diana Bonet discusses four behavioral styles. She writes: No one is just one style. We are combinations of all the styles, but you probably see more of yourself in one style that the others. Often we see other people's styles (co-workers, family, friends) before we recognize our own. Don't get locked in here. This information has real value in helping you to understand more clearly your needs and expectations" as a team leader or a team member. The four styles are:

> ➤ **The Promoting Style**

> ➤ **The Directive Style**

> ➤ **The Analytical Style**

> ➤ **The Supportive Style**

Each person's dominant behavior style provides important personality clues, including one's natural communication style. The pages that follow outline the main characteristics of each style.

---

*For more information on behavior or personality styles, read *The Business of Listening,* by Diana Bonet, and *Accountability,* by Sam R. Lloyd, both by Crisp Publications.

The Promoting Style

The Good Stuff: These folks are peppy! They have lots of energy and they get excited about things. Their positive, outgoing nature motivates everyone. As team members, promoters see the "big picture." They are inventive, confident, and idealistic about reaching goals. In meetings they keep things stirred up by cracking jokes and injecting ideas (even when they are not asked for). Their promoting style is sociable and fun to be around.

The Downside: Promoters are always on the leading edge with new ideas, but they are not good at following through. They prefer to leave the grunt work to someone else. They tend to over-promise, which often causes them to be late. A promoter's computer screen saver might read: "Deadlines amuse me." Some people see promoters as superficial because they move so quickly from idea to idea without following through. They also appear to be disorganized.

Do you think this is your style? ❏ Yes ❏ No

Identify someone famous who has strong tendencies to be a promoter:

_____

Someone on your team or in your work environment:

_____

Someone in your personal life:

_____

What can a promoter bring to your team?

_____

How can you use the strengths of a promoter to help your team?

_____

How might the downside characteristics affect your team?

_____

What steps might you want to take to avoid the downside problems?

_____

The Directive Style

The Good Stuff: Like a human bulldozer, the directive style plows through obstacles, ignores excuses, and gets things done. This unemotional, take-charge style approaches problems realistically and boldly. Within your team, directives will dominate and control because of their forceful manner. With a directive, winning is everything. These hard chargers do not waste time and money, and they are realistic about both. When situations get tough, they tighten controls. They value achievement and expect big rewards (money, yachts, islands). Their screen saver might say, "What's the bottom line?"

The Downside: Directives are not humble. They have big egos and they play to win. They seldom praise or give credit to others. Sometimes they are downright critical and insensitive. They expect a lot, and they are critical and demanding when they do not get results. Generally they are not good listeners.

Do you think this is your style?   ❑ Yes ❑ No

Identify someone famous who has strong tendencies to be a directive:

_____

Someone on your team or in your work environment:

_____

Someone in your personal life:

_____

What can a directive bring to your team?

_____

How can you use the strengths of a directive to help your team?

_____

How might the downside characteristics affect your team?

_____

What steps might you want to take to avoid the downside problems?

_____

The Analytical Style

The Good Stuff: This style is, above all, logical. Analyticals are usually neat, organized, and precise, and they lean toward professions that require these qualities—engineering, science, accounting, and research. As excellent problem solvers, they contribute to their work teams with a thorough knowledge of the subject, an objective analysis of available information, and a practical game plan. They keep agreements and meet deadlines on time. They are dependable and patient. And did we mention logical?!

The Downside: With so many positive qualities, it is hard to imagine a downside to this style. But some would say that rightness can turn quickly to self-righteousness, and insistence on complete accuracy soon becomes tedious and boring. Stubbornness becomes an art form, and the push for perfection can make analyticals ever so picky about the smallest details. Their screen saver might read: "I'm right. I'm right. I'm right."

Do you think this is your style?   ❑ Yes ❑ No

Identify someone famous who has strong tendencies to be an analytical:

_____

Someone on your team or in your work environment:

_____

Someone in your personal life:

_____

What can an analytical bring to your team?

_____

How can you use the strengths of an analytical to help your team?

_____

How might the downside characteristics affect your team?

_____

What steps might you want to take to avoid the downside problems?

_____

The Supportive Style

The Good Stuff: These folks give new meaning to the word "nice." Their friendly, helpful style makes them the ultimate team players. They are easygoing and spontaneous, and they take things as they come. They prefer to work in groups and make decisions by consensus. Their decisions are based on the effects their actions will have on others. In meetings supportives are peacemakers who seek to make co-workers comfortable and happy. Their screen saver might say, "How may I help you?"

The Downside: Because of their need for acceptance, supporting styles do not always say what they think. They will vacillate to please people. They do not do well at setting personal goals. They would rather help other people reach their goals. Individuals of this style operate more on feelings than facts, and they fight with feelings too. More forceful styles see supporting styles as easy marks because they cannot say "No". Supportives also tend to waste time because they are very social, and they often do not take the initiative to get things done.

Do you think this is your style? ❑ Yes ❑ No

Identify someone famous who has strong tendencies to be a supportive:

_____

Someone on your team or in your work environment: (1 line follows)
Someone in your personal life:

_____

What can a supportive bring to your team?

_____

How can you use the strengths of a supportive to help your team?

_____

How might the downside characteristics affect your team?

_____

What steps might you want to take to avoid the downside problems?

_____

Engaging the Strengths of Each Style

People often ask which is the right style. There is no right style. We all have different strengths that we bring to the work environment. The key is to use each individual's strengths and keep from assigning or delegating a task that would not be a fit for that person.

If the team was nearing completion and you wanted to plan a celebration, the promoter would an ideal person to come up with ideas for ways to celebrate. You would not want to put directives in charge. They would think it was a waste of time, and they would already be thinking of the next project for the team to work on. It would also be a good idea to add a supportive to the celebration team to make sure the promoter followed through on the details for the celebration. Using individuals' strengths makes it easier for everyone to accomplish their goals.

In which style did you see yourself the most?

_____

What do you think is the best quality that you bring to the team?

_____

How can the team best use your strengths to help achieve team goals?

_____

_____

Is the team using your strengths to the fullest? ❑ Yes ❑ No

If your answer is no, how could you work to better use your strength?

_____

_____

Building Tip

"To find out what one is fitted to do, and to secure an opportunity to do it, is the key to happiness."

–John Dewey

Building a Solid Team Through Training

An essential part of an efficient team is effective training. When people have the tools and knowledge to do their jobs well, then everyone succeeds—the employee, the team, and the organization. To build a well-rounded team, it is important to provide training of various types to accommodate different individuals and needs.

Classroom Training

Classroom training can be a valuable team-building tool. Topics such as selling, customer service, and listening demand that people interact with one another. If there is an area in which your entire team could use improvement, a training class might just be the answer. It would give team members an opportunity to build their skills in a safe environment. Spending time together—whether a half day, full day, or multiple days—enables team members to get to know one another and build trust.

On-the-Job Training

On-the-job training is another useful tool. Empowering people to share their knowledge helps them continue to build connections and relationships. Peer training, when done correctly, can be rewarding for both the trainer and the trainee. The worst kind of on-the-job training, however, is unstructured and impromptu, as in, "George, show Mike how to do this."

Effective training is well designed and implemented. Both the trainer and the trainee understand the learning objectives, the learning activities that will take place, and how learning will be measured. Ideally, materials (a participant guide, trainer's guide, and any learning aides) are provided to maintain consistency.

Online or Computer-Based Training

With the accessibility of technology through the Internet, CD-ROM, and DVD, more training can be conducted through computers. The flexibility that technology provides allows employees to go through training at the time and pace they choose. Such learning is best for technical skills that can be practiced and measured through the computer, such as writing, budgeting, scheduling, and other "hard" skills.

By reading information, watching video, doing practices, and taking tests, employees can gather the information they need to do their jobs well. Many companies also use online or computer-based training as a way to prepare students for classroom training. By completing an online module before class, employees can come prepared with the information they need, then use classroom time for review and practice.

Evaluating Training Programs

For any form of training you provide, make sure it meets these criteria:

➤ **Useful**
All programs must be relevant and meet employee needs. If training classes are seen as a waste of time, employees will fail to participate even in necessary training.

➤ **Ongoing**
Many organizations fail to build successful teams because the only training employees get is when they are first hired. Ongoing training will keep employees interested and meet their development needs.

➤ **Effective**
Designing training to be effective is not a skill possessed by everyone. Do not make the mistake of thinking that subject-matter experts are necessarily equipped to do the training! Well-designed learning materials can be purchased or developed in-house. Either way, use your resources wisely to make sure people are learning what they need to know.

➤ **Interesting and Enjoyable**
It is safe to assume that not many people enjoy sitting in a conference room listening to someone talk about a subject ad nauseum. Find ways to appeal to your participants by including activities, discussion, and sprucing up the environment. Make what they have learned applicable back on the job. Combine training formats (classroom, on-the-job, and online) to appeal to different styles and maintain employee interest.

Training is a great way to build your team and support continued growth. Periodically evaluate your team's training needs and provide team members with opportunities to participate in training, both as a trainee and as a facilitator, when appropriate.

The suggestions on the next page will help you assess your current approach to training.

For more information on developing effective training, read *50 One-Minute Tips for Trainers* by Carrie Van Daele, and *Training Managers to Train* by Brother Herman Zaccarelli, both by Crisp Publications.

HOW SUPPORTIVE OF TRAINING ARE YOU?

Your attitude, knowledge, and approach will influence what is learned in your training program and how well it is applied. The following suggestions will help you improve your return on investment in training.

Place a check mark (✔) if you already do what is suggested and an X if you plan to begin this practice.

I normally:

❑ Review performance against expectations periodically with each employee and jointly identify training that will strengthen results.

❑ Listen to an employee's growth objectives and support them when it is appropriate to do so.

❑ Talk in advance to employees selected for training to reinforce the training's importance to their job.

❑ Have employees' work covered by others while they are in training so they can concentrate on what is being taught.

❑ Help employees develop an action plan to apply their training to the job.

❑ Ask employees for an evaluation of the training program and whether it would be suitable for other members of the team.

❑ Assign work to employees that allows them to apply new techniques and methods they learned during training.

❑ Compliment employees when they apply their newly acquired skills.

Promoting Teamwork Through Your Management Style

To help focus your team's efforts on achieving organizational goals, you must put a strong dose of leadership into the way you work with your team—your management style. Everyone likes to work for a leader who makes it possible to stay motivated and headed in the right direction. Just as professional athletes build loyalty toward coaches who lead them to a championship, people on your team will like to work for someone who leads them to achieve first-rate results.

The following are three approaches to management. Which best fits you?

➤ *"I know best."*

This manager believes work gets done by controlling the people who do it. Employees are told what to do, how to do it, and when to stop. Then they are told what they did wrong and what they did right, where they are weak and where they are strong. The "I know best" manager feels this is justified because of her superior knowledge and ability.

But this attitude does not invite new ideas, challenge people, or stimulate a cooperative, supportive spirit. Communication is directed one way only.

➤ *"I'll set the goals, you meet them."*

This person feels that because of his superior knowledge, ability, or experience, it is okay to establish goals for others to meet. The employee is given an opportunity to discuss ways to meet goals but has no input into performance objectives. When this happens, commitment is more difficult to obtain from employees because their lack of involvement precludes a sense of ownership.

➤ *"Let's review the work together, establish realistic goals, and evaluate performance accordingly."*

This leader emphasizes work performance, not authoritarian control. The idea is to first communicate organizational needs, then help team members contribute their ideas. The leader acts as a resource and enabler rather than as a judge. Communication is open and flows in both directions. The value of mutual support and cooperation is recognized and employed.

Which management style did you check as being most like you? Obviously, the most effective management style involves working together to establish and meet goals, and these topics are addressed in Part 4.

Building Tip

"Hold yourself responsible for a higher standard than anybody expects of you. Never excuse yourself."

–Henry Ward Beecher

For more information on supervisory skills, read *The New Supervisor,* by Elwood N. Chapman and Wil McKnight, Crisp Publications.

CASE STUDY: THE COMPLAINING EMPLOYEES

Joyce and Sue work in computer services under Kimberly's supervision. They are both depressed about their jobs and have been complaining to each other.

Joyce is unhappy because she was never given her job description and has only a limited understanding of what is expected of her. When she asked Kimberly about it, she was told, "Don't worry, I'll keep you busy." Joyce never receives a new assignment until she completes the previous one she was assigned. Sometimes a day or more will pass before Kimberly is able to give Joyce a new project. Recently Joyce started helping a co-worker because she had nothing else to do. Kimberly later told her: "Don't do that again. Assigning the work is my responsibility." Joyce has since been criticized by her co-workers for not pitching in when they are busy and she is not.

Sue, on the other hand, is concerned about the backlog building up in her job. The problem has occurred because of repeated changes in project objectives, which were not communicated until after a critical point in the work affected had passed. Kimberly insists on handling all communications with other groups their department serves. Because Kimberly is so busy, however, she frequently fails to pass along important information to Sue and is equally slow in getting answers from Sue that others need.

Are Sue's and Joyce's complaints justified? ❏ Yes ❏ No
Support your position:

_____

_____

_____

Compare your answers to the authors' responses in the back of the book.

Installing Windows
to Better
Communication

Facilitating Open Communication

Now that the team framework is in place, you must concentrate on building an atmosphere conducive to open communication and cooperation not only within your team, but also between your team and other units of the organization. So the next step is to install the "windows" that will help everyone keep communication open.

Research shows the best leaders are those that have learned to give clear instructions, stay responsive to questions and suggestions, and keep the appropriate parties well informed. Research also confirms a positive correlation between communication (understanding) and:

➤ Improved productivity

➤ Better problem solving

➤ A reduction in grievances

➤ Ideas for improvement in methodology

➤ Improved working relationships

➤ Greater personal satisfaction

Two-Way Communication

Team leaders use communication to gather, process, and transmit information essential to the well-being of the organization. They are the pivotal people who must carefully consider the information needs of many because they respond to questions and provide answers in many directions—to and from peers, superiors, and team members.

In the chart that follows, the left-hand column lists typical questions from the team member's point of view. Team leaders need an entirely different set of questions to respond to the organization's needs. Examples of these are listed in the right-hand column.

Team Member	Team Leader
What information do I need to my superiors?	What information should I pass up from above?
Where should I get it?	How should it be conveyed?
When should I get it?	How often is it required?
What groups can provide specific information on policy and procedure?	What groups depend on me for information?
How do I get it?	To whom do I give the information?
What do they expect from me?	When do I give them information?
What information should I get from people working with me?	How do I provide the information?
How should I get it?	What do employees working for me want to know?
How often?	How do I provide it?
What should I do with it?	When do I get someone else to provide it?

Team Building

...ommunications by including many 'windows.' Effec-
...ommunications are transparent. Hidden agendas
...rust."

—Mike Foti

REVIEW YOUR COMMUNICATION SKILLS

Complete each of the following statements by circling the more appropriate choice.

1. Messages are most easily understood when:
   (a) You use your full command of the language
   (b) They are sent in terms the receiver understands

2. Complex information is more easily understood when you:
   (a) Improve clarity by using specific examples and analogies
   (b) Tell the listener to pay careful attention

3. Key concepts are better remembered when you:
   (a) Use repetition to reinforce them
   (b) Express yourself clearly

4. Organizing a message before transmitting it:
   (a) Often takes more time than it is worth
   (b) Makes it easier to understand

5. The sender can determine the receiver's understanding by:
   (a) Asking if he understands
   (b) Asking the receiver to report what he heard

6. Listening is more effective when you:
   (a) Concentrate on the sender and what is being said
   (b) Anticipate what the speaker is going to say

7. Understanding is easier when you:
   (a) Suspend judgment until the sender finishes the message
   (b) Assume you know the sender's position and judge accordingly

8. Understanding can be improved by the listener's:
   (a) Periodically paraphrasing the message back to the sender
   (b) Interrupting to express feelings and emotions

CONTINUED

9. Good listeners:
    (a) Have their response ready when the sender stops talking
    (b) Ask questions when they don't understand

10. Sending and receiving are both enhanced when:
    (a) The parties maintain good eye contact
    (b) The parties are defensive and challenge each other

Building Tip

Encourage team members to review communications skills using this exercise. Then compare notes and discuss how to improve. This will be another cooperative step in building a stronger team effort.

Answers: 1(b); 2(a); 3(a); 4(b); 5(b); 6(a); 7(a); 8(a); 9(b); 10(a).

Fostering Team Commitment Throug; Collaboration

Supervisors cannot do it all, no matter how talented and committed
Their success is measured by their ability to delegate intelligently a...
motivate employees to accomplish the organization's goals. A team attains the
highest level of achievement when it is committed to the task and fully uses each
member's talents.

Commitment cannot be forced. It is self-generating and usually develops through
a sense of involvement and collaboration. People increase commitment to a team
when they are allowed to contribute to its success. They feel more important and
needed when they feel a responsibility for results. Once team members are
actively involved in goal setting and problem solving, they develop a sense of
ownership. They can effectively pursue team goals, much like an entrepreneur
does.

Increased Effectiveness from Collaboration

Working together to achieve common goals, team members stimulate each other
to higher levels of accomplishment. Fresh ideas are generated and tested, and the
team's productivity exceeds any combined efforts of employees working indi-
vidually. In this way, collaboration builds interdependence. People recognize the
benefits of helping one another and realize it is expected.

People collaborating on teams gain personal power in the form of confidence
from knowing that others share their views and are acting in concert with them.
Team goals become individual goals, and group problems become individual
problems. Members contribute their best to problem solving because they have a
personal stake in doing so. The effort is non-threatening.

When members help design the systems and methods used by the team, they
have the opportunity to see the effect of their effort and the efforts of others on
achievement. They understand why controls are important and make a commitment to support them. This is especially true when members know it is possible
to revise or improve controls when required.

Collaboration also helps team members satisfy their participative needs. It helps
build a framework in which individual needs can be learned, understood, and
supported by all.

Encouraging Collaboration on Your Team

The benefits of collaboration make it easy to understand why managers who foster such teamwork are considered leaders. You can encourage and support collaboration in the following ways:

➤ Identify areas of interdependence that make collaboration appropriate. Involve team members in planning and problem solving to help them identify where collaboration is needed.

➤ Keep lines of communication open among everyone involved in a problem, project, or course of action.

➤ Let the team know in advance that teamwork will positively influence individual recognition.

Building Tip

A supervisor controls the degree to which employees are involved. Open up opportunities for participation and watch the commitment grow.

Involving the Team in Setting Goals and Standards

Team goals and standards should be established with the participation of those responsible for meeting them. After all, well-selected, trained employees should know more about what is achievable than anyone else.

Before taking a look at how team members can help establish goals and standards, however, let's define the two terms, as follows:

➤ *Goals* are statements of results to be achieved. They describe:
- Conditions that will exist when the desired outcome has been accomplished
- A time frame during which the outcome is to be completed
- Resources the organization is willing to commit to achieving the desired result

➤ *Standards* refer to ongoing performance criteria. Usually expressed quantitatively, standards may include:
- Attendance
- Breakage
- Manufacturing tolerances
- Production rates
- Safety standards

Goal-Setting Roles for Team Members and Leaders

Like other critical skills, goal setting may take practice. An effective way for the team to work together to establish goals and standards and the action plans to achieve them is by filling the roles as outlined below.

Team Member	Leader
Helps establish performance goals and standards. This is a "self-contract" for achievement and a commitment to deliver a result for the team.	Ensures team goals are achievable but challenging enough to meet organizational needs and provide a sense of accomplishment.
Develops methods to measure results and checkpoints for control purposes.	Helps balance the complexity of measures and controls with value received.
Outlines the action required to accomplish goals and standards.	Participates with the team to test the action plan's validity against alternatives.
Specifies participation required from colleagues or other units within the organization.	Reviews what cooperation and support are required and helps obtain them if necessary.
Reports progress as work is performed. Seeks guidance and assistance when needed. Adjusts plan as required.	Follows the progress of the work. Reinforces achievement and assists in problem solving when indicated. Ensures targets are met, or modified if circumstances so indicate.

Building Tip

These roles place the responsibility for performance on the appropriate team members and provide the latitude to achieve results. The leader concentrates on being a challenger, prober, coach, and enabler.

Making Problem Solving a Team Effort

Problems inevitably arise in any team effort, but many supervisors spend too much time trying to solve problems that could better be handled by the team members themselves. When supervisors feel responsible for solving all the problems, production is slowed, employees are frustrated, and personal growth is limited. The supervisor ends up with less time to plan, organize, motivate, and control.

Team effectiveness is more easily achieved when the supervisor simply participates in problem solving rather than dominating it. The example on the next page illustrates this concept.

The Case of the Missing Keys

Renee, the nursing supervisor, was frustrated. The employees were constantly losing or misplacing the keys to the medicine cart. Each shift would have several sets of keys and then they were to pass the keys to the next shift. The problem was keys were often left in uniform pockets and taken home or they were simply lost.

Renee was determined to solve the problem. Too much time was spent looking for the keys, and there was always the possibility the keys could fall into the wrong hands. A duplicate set of keys could not be made because of the drugs involved, so the cart would have to be re-keyed, which would be expensive.

Renee drafted a memo about the problem for all three shifts to review for possible ideas. She also asked each shift nurse to discuss possible solutions during the shift meetings.

The nurses had a wide variety of ideas. Some wanted the nursing supervisor to be responsible for the keys. One nurse recounted that in another facility where she had worked, the keys were always visible on the uniforms.

The system they implemented was two-fold. They decided to purchase brightly colored spiral wristbands to hold the keys. The second part involved designing a system in which the nurse who had the keys would sign them in and out.

The nurses liked the keys hooked to the bright-colored bands, but some found them to be too cumbersome on their wrists so they pinned the bands to their uniforms instead. The sign-in system also made it much easier to track down missing keys. The problem of the missing and lost keys dramatically decreased.

Renee used her problem-solving skills to find a solution for a serious problem. She also used the insight of the staff involved in the problem to help find a new system. Renee's problem gave the facility a new framework for its work procedure involving the keys to the medicine cart.

Building Tip

Involve the people who have a vested interest for greater ownership and accountability.

Seven Steps to Solving Problems

Problem solving should be taught at every level of an organization. The process should be as simple as is required to get the job done. A basic approach is outlined below. Check (✔) those steps that would be useful in your operation.

❑   **Step 1**   **State what appears to be the problem.**
    The real problem may not surface until facts have been gathered and analyzed. Therefore, start with a supposition that can later be confirmed or corrected.

❑   **Step 2**   **Gather facts, feelings, and opinions.**
    What happened? Where, when, and how did the problem occur? What is its size, scope, and severity? Who and what is affected? Is it likely to happen again? Does it need to be corrected? Time and expense may require problem solvers to think through what they need and assign priorities to the more critical elements.

❑   **Step 3**   **Restate the problem.**
    The facts help make this possible and provide supporting data. The actual problem may or may not be the same as stated in Step 1.

❑   **Step 4**   **Identify alternative solutions.**
    Generate ideas. Do not eliminate any possible solutions until several have been discussed.

❑   **Step 5**   **Evaluate alternatives.**
    Which will provide the optimum solution? What are the risks? Are costs in keeping with the benefits? Will the solution create new problems?

❑   **Step 6**   **Implement the decision.**
    Who must be involved? To what extent? How, when, and where? Who will the decision affect? What might go wrong? How will results be reported and verified?

❑   **Step 7**   **Evaluate the results.**
    Test the solution against the desired results. Modify the solution if better results are needed.

Creating a Climate for Team Problem Solving

A team involved in problem solving can obtain improved results by using sound group processes. This means team members commit to finding the best possible solution to a problem rather than imposing their exclusive view. The leader participates as a team member and is subject to the same rules. Open communication is expected, and team members are encouraged to challenge ideas to test their usefulness in solving the problem. A successful solution from a group is often far more effective than single solutions offered by individuals.

The following conditions support good team problem solving. Check (✔) those now existing in your team and place an X by those you want to add.

❑ Team members readily contribute from their experience and listen to the contributions of others.

❑ Conflicts arising from different points of view are considered helpful and are resolved constructively by the team.

❑ Team members challenge suggestions they believe are unsupported by facts or logic but avoid arguing just to have their way.

❑ Poor solutions are not supported just for the sake of harmony or agreement.

❑ Differences of opinion are discussed and resolved. Coin tossing, averaging, majority vote, and similar cop-outs are avoided when making a decision.

❑ Every team member strives to make the problem-solving process efficient and is careful to facilitate rather than hinder discussion.

❑ Team members encourage and support co-workers who may be reluctant to offer ideas.

❑ Team members understand the value of time and work to eliminate extraneous or repetitious discussion.

❑ Team decisions are not arbitrarily overruled by the leader simply because she does not agree with them.

❑ The team understands that the leader will make the best decision he can, if a satisfactory team solution is not forthcoming.

Building Tip

"It takes a great man [or woman] to be a good listener."

—Calvin Coolidge

Examining Conflict

As you have seen in the preceding list of conditions for team problem solving, conflict inevitably can arise from differing points of view. Indeed, team leaders must accept that any time two or more people are brought together, the stage is set for potential conflict, as in the following examples:

➤ Some members of Memorial Church want to use church funds to aid the local poor. Others prefer spending more money for missionary work. Still others think new carpeting for the sanctuary is the greatest need.

➤ A sales manager wants a large inventory of all products, so quick deliveries to customers can be promised. The manufacturing manager wants to limit the inventory to hold down storage costs.

In both of these situations all parties mean well and if questioned would maintain they were trying to accomplish what they perceived to be the best objective. Nonetheless, conflict is present because of:

➤ Differences in needs, objectives, and values

➤ Differences in perceiving motives, words, actions, and situations

➤ Differing expectations of outcomes—favorable vs. unfavorable

➤ Unwillingness to work through issues, to collaborate or compromise

Building Tip

"Examine what is said, not him who speaks."

—Arab Proverb

Conflict Resolution Styles

When conflict does occur, the results may be positive or negative depending on how those involved choose to approach it. With this in mind, team leaders must realize that positive contributions can arise from conflict, providing it does not get out of control.

There are five basic approaches to conflict resolution, as summarized in the following chart.

Style	Characteristic Behavior	User Justification
Avoidance	Nonconfrontational. Ignores or passes over issues. Denies issues are a problem.	Differences too minor or too great to resolve. Attempts might damage relationships or create even greater problems.
Accommodating	Agreeable, nonassertive behavior. Cooperative even at the expense of personal goals.	Not worth risking damage to relationships or general disharmony.
Win/Lose	Confrontational, assertive, and aggressive. Must win at any cost.	Survival of the fittest. Must prove superiority. Most ethically or professionally correct.
Compromising	Important for all parties to achieve basic goals and maintain good relationships. Aggressive but cooperative.	No one person or idea is perfect. There is more than one good way to do anything. You must give to get.
Problem Solving	Needs of both parties are legitimate and important. High respect for mutual support. Assertive and cooperative.	When parties will openly discuss issues, a mutually beneficial solution can be found without making a major concession.

As you can see from the chart, conflict becomes unhealthy when it is avoided or approached on a win/lose basis. Animosities develop, communications break down, trust and mutual support deteriorate, and hostilities result. When sides are chosen, productivity diminishes or stops. The damage is usually difficult (sometimes impossible) to repair.

Helping the Team Resolve Conflict Positively

Teaching team members to understand conflict and resolve it positively will help the team succeed. You and your team may find the following diagram helpful in discussing conflict resolution styles.

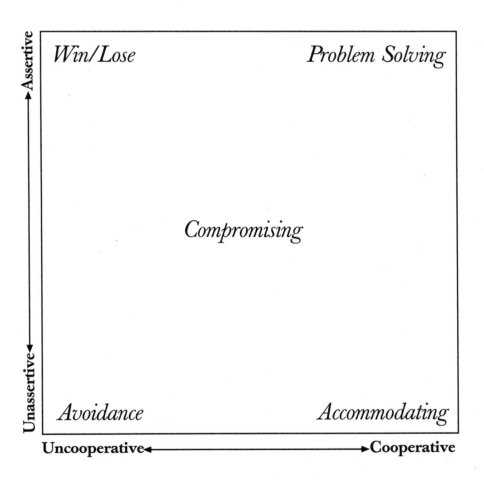

Indicate with an "F" the style you are most likely to use with followers, a "P" with your peers, and an "S" with your supervisor. Review the preceding chart and this diagram with team members and test one another's perceptions. Discuss ways conflicts can be more effectively resolved in the team and with other units. Then answer the questions on the next page.

58

1. Which style is the most uncooperative and least assertive?

_____

2. Which style is characterized by assertive behavior yet represents the maximum in cooperation?

_____

3. Which style is cooperative but unassertive?

_____

4. Which style is assertive and uncooperative?

_____

5. Which style takes the middle ground on assertiveness and cooperation?

_____

Building Tip

Conflict is healthy when it causes the parties to explore new ideas, test their position and beliefs, and stretch their imagination. When conflict is dealt with constructively, people can be stimulated to greater creativity, which leads to a wider variety of alternatives and better results.

Answers to questions 1 through 5: 1. Avoidance; 2. Problem Solving; 3. Accommodating; 4. Win/Lose; 5. Compromising.

CASE STUDY: CONFLICTING TEAM MEMBERS

When team members understand the nature of conflict and constructive methods to resolve it, they can usually work out disagreements themselves. When they cannot, or when the problem requires your intervention for other reasons, you may have to engineer a solution. How would you solve this conflict?

Tara is supervisor of a small group of quality-control testers in a chemical-products laboratory. At different times, two testers have come to her with different suggestions for reporting test results to plant operations. The first, Jeremy, wants to send the results to the foreman in charge of the unit where the samples were produced. Angela, on the other hand, wants to send the reports directly to the lead operator on the unit so corrective changes can be made as soon as possible.

Angela and Jeremy are both good people but very competitive. Tara is aware they have already exchanged a few sharp remarks over the issue. Both ideas are reasonable and either is better than the current practice of sending reports to the administrative office.

CONTINUED

From the list below, select the approach to conflict resolution used in each option and write it in the blank provided. Then indicate with a check (✔) the approach you would use if you were Tara.

Win/lose   Avoidance   Accommodation
Compromising   Problem Solving

❑ 1. _____ Study the situation independently, decide who is right, and tell Jeremy and Angela to implement your decision.

❑ 2. _____ Wait to see what happens.

❑ 3. _____ Let each handle the reporting in his or her own way.

❑ 4. _____ Get Jeremy and Angela together to work out a solution they can both live with even though they must both give a little.

❑ 5. _____ Suggest Jeremy and Angela combine their ideas so that both can achieve their goals (send the report to the foreman with a copy to the lead operator).

Compare your answers with the authors' responses in the back of the book.

Erecting a Stable

Roof of Trust

62

Building Trust Within the Team

In our team-building process, we are ready to put the roof on. Just as a house roof protects it from the elements, the "roof" you will apply in this process—trust—will protect you and your team.

As people work toward building their team, they get to know one another. They learn to respect individual differences, appreciate team contributions, and enjoy the satisfaction that teamwork provides when both personal and organizational goals are achieved.

Trust is an essential part of this experience because of the powerful effect it has on every aspect of team performance. The trust that is built in the work environment is a form of protection for the team members.

Elements of Trust

When leading workshops, the original author of this book, Robert Maddux, would ask his participants to collaborate in writing down their feelings about trust. The following are the responses of individuals who learned team-building techniques.

Individual	
A	"To build trust it is essential to have clearly and consistently administered goals that contain employee input. Employees must perceive their managers as open, fair, honest, and willing to listen. Managers must be decisive and stand by their decisions in difficult situations." "Employees must have the confidence that their manager will support them, even in delicate matters, and take responsibility for group actions. A manager must also readily give credit to employees where credit is due."
B	"I define trust as an assured reliance on the character, ability, and strength or truth of someone or something. Trust is built in a work group by promoting open communications, providing fair leadership, and supervising with sensitivity."
C	"Establishing trust in a work group requires open and honest communication, accepting others, sharing a common goal, and respecting the opinions of others on how to achieve that goal."
D	"Trust is necessary to have a productive working environment. It is essential for all personnel to practice open, honest communication to increase awareness and build cooperation. This environment of trust promotes loyalty and commitment to achieve the organization's goals and objectives."

Recognizing Employees for a Job Well Done

Team performance can be improved when members receive feedback on how well they are doing. Positive recognition when things are done right encourages similar performance in the future. One of the most powerful forms of recognition is praise.

Some managers use praise effectively; others use it poorly or not at all. Many team leaders or managers simply do not understand the importance of showing their employees appreciation. Some think, "They work for the company, not me personally. Why should I thank them?"

But the book, *Retaining Your Employees,* advocates, "Acknowledging employees is a major part of recognition." Employees want to know they are an important part of the team, so it is important to provide them with specific, sincere, and down-to-earth feedback. The chart that follows contrasts the differences in feedback styles between successful and unsuccessful team leaders.

Which Team Leader Will You Be?

Successes	Failures
Leaders who think it important to help people feel good about themselves.	Those who are insensitive to the needs of others.
Leaders who give periodic praise to team members for meeting job requirements.	Those who think praise is improper for persons who meet, but do not exceed, job requirements.
Leaders who understand that people respond better to praise for what they do well than to criticism for what they do wrong.	Those who look only for what is being done wrong and consistently give only negative feedback.
Leaders who give sincere praise for reasons the receiver can understand.	Those who are insincere and use praise only to get something they want.
Leaders who praise teamwork but also recognize individual contributions to final results.	Those who do not go to the trouble to reward teamwork or identify individual contributions.
Add from your own experience: _____ _____ _____ _____	Add from your own experience: _____ _____ _____ _____

Building Tip _____

Praise given when earned rewards the giver as well as the receiver.

For more information on providing recognition, read *Retaining Your Employees,* by Barb Wingfield and Janice Berry, Crisp Publications.

Implementing Positive Discipline

As you have just learned, acknowledging employees for a job well done encourages similar performance in the future. But corrective action also can set the stage for future success by clearing the air and redirecting inappropriate or inadequate performance. Discipline is a basic requirement of team performance. A good leader maintains control but strives to establish an environment in which team members exercise self-control. This is accomplished by following through on the true meaning of discipline—namely, "training that develops or molds by instruction or exercise."

The means by which positive discipline can be implemented are listed below. This process, when consistently applied and followed, will eliminate most disciplinary problems.

Indicate your proficiency by checking (✔)the appropriate box.

Do Well	Should Improve	
❏	❏	1. From the outset, make sure team members understand what is expected of them and what standards are to be met.
❏	❏	2. Teach team members how to fulfill expectations and achieve standards.
❏	❏	3. Encourage team members as they make progress toward attaining company goals.
❏	❏	4. Compliment team members when standards are achieved and expectations are realized.
❏	❏	5. Redirect inadequate or inappropriate performance when it occurs, and repeat Steps 1-4.
❏	❏	6. If the inadequate or inappropriate performance persists after a reasonable period of time (and Step 5 has been applied), evaluate the person's role on the team.

Building Tip

Did you know that for every one corrective comment or suggestion, you must provide five positive comments? This ratio applies over time, not in just one interaction with a person—and not only in work situations, but also in personal relationships.

Coaching: A Key Ingredient in Team Building

Forming a team, developing the personal skills of its members, and enabling them to work together effectively are essential steps in team building. But this effort must be sustained by continuous analysis of results and corresponding adjustments in member contributions and the game plan to meet changing objectives. The team leader, therefore, must be an adept coach who is constantly improving and applying coaching techniques to meet the needs of the situation and the team.

Helping as a Function of Supervision

Managers not only must realize that helping is a basic function of supervision, but also must let team members know that they are available and want to help. Sometimes this help comes as reassurance and empathy. Sometimes it just involves listening and reflecting. Most important, coaching means challenging people, delegating responsibilities, and giving people opportunities to get involved and to grow and develop by learning from their own successes and mistakes.

Managers who are committed to coaching see this function not as a luxury to be carried out when time permits, but as a necessity. They have experienced the results that occur when employees are encouraged to work to their full potential. They have enjoyed the increased productivity and appreciated the strengthening of their organization as individuals have begun to demonstrate their competence and improve their contribution to the team.

Influencing Others Toward Achievement

Few people who achieve a position of leadership can truly claim sole responsibility for their accomplishment. Someone helped them—someone who knew the individual and the goals of the organization and who was willing to devote effort to achieving both. This action may have been so subtle, so natural, so well organized, or so well woven into the fabric of the relationship that it is visible only in retrospect. Managers who have this kind of positive impact on other team members recognize that the helping relationship is fundamental to the development of a strong organization.

In their role of helping people grow and adjust to change, managers provide guidance and support. But they also realize that employees must help themselves too. Thus, coaching can be seen as the skylight in the roof that allows employees to see a larger, broader vision for themselves.

Building Tip

Praise in public, criticize in private.

SPHERES OF INFLUENCE

Most managers can identify people who have influenced their lives in some way—parents, friends, teachers, associates, or supervisors. Sometimes this influence has been profound, perhaps even changing the course of their lives.

Think about these influences in your life and answer the questions in the spaces provided.

Who influenced you?

_____   _____
_____   _____
_____   _____
_____   _____

In what way(s) were you influenced?

_____
_____
_____

Who influences you now?

_____   _____
_____   _____
_____   _____
_____   _____

In what way(s) do they influence you?

_____
_____
_____

=CONTINUED=

═CONTINUED═

Whom do you influence?

_____   _____

_____   _____

_____   _____

_____   _____

What outcomes do you have the power to influence?

_____

_____

WHAT IS YOUR ATTITUDE TOWARD COACHING?

Coaching offers one of the best opportunities you have to leave a positive imprint on individual team members, your team as a whole, and the organization. Some managers consider the coaching aspects of their jobs the most rewarding and lasting contributions they can make in the work setting.

What is your attitude toward coaching? Check (✔) the column below first to reflect your past attitude toward coaching. Then, after contemplating what you have learned from your experience and from reading this book, reflect what you anticipate your future attitude toward coaching will be.

Coaching Applications	Former Attitude Toward Coaching			Future Attitude Toward Coaching		
	Essential	Useful	Waste of time	Essential	Useful	Waste of time
Coaching is vital to shaping employee performance in the current assignment.						
Coaching enables employees to learn more quickly and reach their level of competence more rapidly.						
Coaching provides a way to help employees achieve their potential as well as tailor that potential to support the skills of other team members.						
Employees accept and adapt more quickly to change when coaching involves them in the process and guides them through.						
Coaching following performance feedback improves the likelihood of positive results.						

Six Tools for Effective Coaching

From increased performance to improved morale, your team's success depends on your learning the skills to become a better coach to your team members. In today's ever-changing work environment, a manager must have the tools to coach employees to meet demanding and changing job responsibilities.

In her book, *Coaching for Development,* Marianne Minor presents six tools that managers must use to discover and encourage their employees' potential: listening, observing, analyzing, interviewing, contracting, and giving feedback. Here is a brief description of each essential tool:

➤ **Listening**
- Pay attention to the employee
- Make eye contact, minimize distractions, and demonstrate open body posture
- Paraphrase what employees say and ask open-ended questions
- Pay attention to body posture and nonverbal signals
- Summarize at the end of the discussion

➤ **Observing**
- Look, listen, watch, and wait for cues from employees for when they need more help or can take more responsibility
- Watch for changes in performance
- Observe employees in various situations
- Look for opportunities to expand competencies, reinforce effective performance, and remove barriers

➤ **Analyzing**
- Know how to determine the root cause of a problem
- Examine the possibilities, whether personal issues, skill deficit, lack of motivation, or boredom
- Assess employees' learning styles and what motivates each person

➤ **Interviewing**
- Formulate useful questions to probe for the employee's skills, values, and accomplishments
- Demonstrate an interviewing style that does not make the employee feel interrogated or defensive
- Ask open-ended questions, closed-ended questions, and reflective questions to fit the situation

> **Contracting**
  • Create a partnership with employees
  • Encourage employees to take responsibility for their careers
  • Include in agreements the who, what, when, how, and other details
    to ensure expectations and commitments will be met

> **Giving Feedback**
  • Tailor the feedback to the employee's skill and knowledge level
  • Be careful not to overload
  • Be specific about observable behavior

Nine Tips for Effective Feedback

1. Be specific when referring to behavior.

2. Consider your timing. Before the event, give feedback in the form of advice; immediately after the event, give positive feedback.

3. Consider the needs of the person receiving the feedback as well as your own. Ask yourself what the person will get out of the information. Are you "dumping" or genuinely attempting to improve performance or the relationship?

4. Focus on the behavior the receiver can do something about.

5. Avoid labels and judgments by describing rather than evaluating behavior.

6. Define the impact on you, the unit, the team, and the company.

7. Use "I statements" to reduce defensiveness.

8. Check to make sure your message has been clearly received.

9. Give the feedback in calm, unemotional words, tone, and body language.

Putting Coaching to Work

Thomas was a new employee with great potential. Amy, his supervisor, was thrilled to have someone new in her department with so much experience in their industry. Amy wanted to put Thomas's expertise to use as quickly as possible but decided first to get his input. She asked him about his previous employment and what he liked and did not like about the work environment. She listened intently as he explained.

Amy continued to observe and analyze Thomas's work style. It seemed that he was not using all of his knowledge. She arranged a meeting with Thomas to discuss his work performance. She asked effective open-ended questions to discover that Thomas was holding back on his knowledge so he would not alienate his new co-workers.

Amy took into account Thomas's needs as well as those of the entire team as she offered Thomas feedback on how he could use more of his knowledge and help the team improve its performance. Amy and Thomas developed a contract for the future of his career, describing how he would track the expectations and commitments of his job and also help the team achieve higher goals.

For more information on coaching, read *Coaching for Development,* by Marianne Minor, Crisp Publications.

RATE YOUR SKILLS AS A COACH

Rate your coaching effectiveness on the following rating scale:

5 = outstanding 4 = very good 3 = satisfactory
2 = needs improvement 1 = poor

To check your ratings, ask your employees to rate you on the same scale.

1. I recognize differences in my staff and coach them accordingly.	5	4	3	2	1
2. I encourage employee suggestions on implementing change.	5	4	3	2	1
3. I encourage employees to solve their own problems.	5	4	3	2	1
4. I make sure individual employees have a continuing understanding of what is expected of them.	5	4	3	2	1
5. I level with employees about their performance.	5	4	3	2	1
6. I help employees prepare for the future.	5	4	3	2	1
7. I know the personal aspirations of each member of my team.	5	4	3	2	1
8. I look for ways to help people grow on the job.	5	4	3	2	1
9. I ask team members to assist one another to learn and to grow.	5	4	3	2	1
10. I do not discourage conflict but I insist it be resolved in a timely manner.	5	4	3	2	1
11. I work hard to ensure that team members understand, respect, and support one another.	5	4	3	2	1

If you scored less than 4 on any of these practices, that is the item(s) you should target for improvement.

S U M M A R Y

Assessing Your Progress

Answer the following true/false questions to review what you have learned.

True   **False**

❑   ❑   1. Team leaders emphasize each member's involvement and expect that person to take responsibility for his contributions.

❑   ❑   2. If you plan to build a strong team and use members' skills to the maximum, there is little need to improve your own skills.

❑   ❑   3. People are more productive when they feel a sense of ownership of the task or of the organization.

❑   ❑   4. When a true team achieves success, so will all of its members.

❑   ❑   5. Selecting qualified people at the outset who work well with others will support team building.

❑   ❑   6. Commitment to accomplishing tasks is the result when a leader involves team members in planning, goal setting, and problem solving.

❑   ❑   7. Team leaders facilitate training of team members and coach them to apply what has been learned.

❑   ❑   8. Teams are more concerned with getting positive results than they are with "turf" considerations.

❑   ❑   9. Trust is a minor factor in most team situations.

❑   ❑   10. Team members need to know anything that affects the work they are performing.

❑   ❑   11. Competition and conflict in a team is healthy if it is properly controlled and quickly resolved.

continued...

True	False	
❑	❑	12. Open communication in a team will promote understanding, recognition of individual differences, and mutual support.
❑	❑	13. Team members participate in decision making but recognize their leader must act on her own if a consensus cannot be reached or if there is a crisis.
❑	❑	14. Successful teams have little need for recognition and praise.
❑	❑	15. Self-control and good discipline are by-products of team building.

Check your answers with the authors' responses in the back of the book.

Ten Ways to Construct a Strong Team

This book has addressed many of the components needed to build a successful team—planning, organization, goals and motivation, people power, problem solving, and so on. Place a check mark (✔) by the statements that you are successfully implementing.

❏ 1. Develop and maintain basic management and leadership skills.

❏ 2. Practice good employee selection techniques.

❏ 3. Discuss expectations or establish goals that have been mutually set.

❏ 4. Plan for the training and development needs of team members.

❏ 5. Advocate, support, and nurture team-building activities.

❏ 6. Involve team members in any activity where they could make a contribution.

❏ 7. Provide and receive feedback from the team.

❏ 8. Do not let conflict and competition get out of control but do not try to eliminate it altogether either.

❏ 9. Recognize and reward the team and its members.

❏ 10. Understand that some team members might not be a fit for the team, and they need to be reassigned.

Reflect on what you have learned—then develop a personal action plan using the guide on the next page.

Developing a Personal Action Building Plan

Think over the material you have read. Review the self-analysis questionnaires. Rethink the case studies and the reinforcement exercises. What have you learned about team building? What did you learn about yourself? How can you apply what you learned? Make a commitment to become a better team player and a more effective team builder by designing a personal action plan to help you accomplish this goal.

The following guide will help you clarify your goals and outline actions required to achieve your goals.

1. My current team-building skills are effective in the following areas:

_____

_____

2. I need to improve my team-building skills in the following areas:

_____

_____

3. My goals for improving my team-building skills are as follows:
   (Be sure they are specific, attainable, and measurable.)

_____

_____

4. These people and resources can help me achieve my goals:

_____

_____

5. The following are my action steps, along with a timetable to accomplish each goal:

_____

_____

Authors' Responses to Case Studies and Exercises

Case Study: Can This Supervisor Be Saved? (page 14)

Mary Lou is in trouble. It will take serious effort to turn things around. It appears that she is trapped by her office and her paperwork. She needs training to develop more competence and confidence as a supervisor. She must learn to manage herself to be able to manage anyone else. Her employees also seem untrained, unsure of themselves, and poorly disciplined. Until they understand their jobs better and recognize the importance of cooperating with each other, chaos will be the result.

Because Mary Lou's group is interdependent, it must work as a team to be successful. Mary Lou must learn and apply team concepts. Specifically, she must become a better leader and supervisor, build the skills and confidence of her employees, establish a better working climate, and institute an appropriate reward system. How to accomplish this is the basis for this book.

Case Study: Which Supervisor Would You Prefer? (Page 24)

It is good that both Morgana and Jeff recognize the importance of clear goals and plans. Employees who have limited knowledge or expertise may appreciate Morgana's approach because they have a great deal to learn. As they learn under Morgana's management, however, they may feel too restricted to share their ideas. And experienced employees may feel that way at the outset. New methods, better products, and simpler ways to achieve objectives might not be forthcoming.

Experienced employees will appreciate Jeff's approach because it provides a needed outlet to contribute. They will feel free to improve group effectiveness while improving their own. Employees with lesser skills will be encouraged to learn so they too can contribute and become more productive. Jeff's employees will appreciate his decision to participate in supervisory training because they will appreciate a manager who knows the basics.

Case Study: The Complaining Employees (Page 40)

Joyce and Sue have good reasons to complain. Joyce wants the opportunity to grow beyond her current tasks. Her efforts to learn what is expected of her have been blocked and she is discouraged having to wait for assignments. It is frustrating for people who want to contribute to be told not to worry about being idle or not to help others unless directed to do so.

Sue is suffering the consequences of poor communication from her supervisor. This is impossible for Sue to correct until Kimberly either opens communication between users and Sue or begins relaying information in a timely manner.

Kimberly appears to be over-controlling her employees by assuming they cannot think for themselves. She is also preventing voluntary attempts by employees to help and support one another. Kimberly needs to reevaluate her approach to supervision and be more open in her dealings with employees. Otherwise, Kimberly will soon be an "ex-manager."

Case Study: Conflicting Team Members (Pages 59-60)

Using a win/lose approach (option 1) takes a problem-solving opportunity away from Angela and Jeremy and makes one of them a loser. *Avoidance* (option 2) leaves two recommendations unresolved. *Accommodation* (option 3) may work, but could be confusing to the operating department. *Compromising* (option 4) might be the best solution in this example because it requires each employee to carefully examine his or her thinking in light of the other's arguments and to work together to reach an agreeable decision. During this process, they may end up using *problem solving* (option 5), because it not only gets the job done, but it also satisfies the recommendation each made originally.

Assessing Your Progress (Pages 79-80)

1. True. Involvement and responsibility are critical to teams.

2. False. You must have strong skills of your own to build a strong team.

3. True. Ownership builds commitment and responsibility.

4. True. Success indicates that all members played their role.

5. True. Good people are the foundation for success.

6. True. You cannot demand commitment or force it.

7. True. Leaders make training useful.

8. True. Productivity, commitment, open communication, and trust are the usual casualties of "turf" wars.

9. False. Trust is one of the most vital ingredients in teams.

10. True. The right information makes the job easier.

11. True. Competition and conflict are stimulating and mind opening.

12. True. Fail to communicate openly and your team will be at risk of failing.

13. True. Timeliness also is important in decision making.

14. False. Recognition and praise are among the strongest motivators.

15. True. People who are committed to a task, a unit, and one another are not apt to create unnecessary problems.

Additional Reading

Bonet, Diana. *The Business of Listening, Third Edition*. Menlo Park, CA: Crisp Publications, 2001.

Cook, Marshall. *Effective Coaching*. NY: McGraw-Hill, 1999.

Hackett, Donald, Ph.D. and Charles Martin, Ph.D. *Facilitation Skills for Team Leaders*. Menlo Park, CA: Crisp Publications, 1993.

Hayes, David K. and Brother Herman Zaccarelli, C.S.C. *Training Managers to Train,* Revised Edition. Menlo Park, CA: Crisp Publications, 1996.

Jude-York, Deborah, Ph.D.; Lauren Davis, M.S.; and Susan Wise, M.A. *Virtual Teaming*. Menlo Park, CA: Crisp Publications, 2000.

Maxwell, John. *The 17 Indisputable Laws of Teamwork*. Nashville, TN: Thomas Nelson Publishers, 2001.

Minor, Marianne. *Coaching for Development*. Menlo Park, CA: Crisp Publications, 1995.

Pokras, Sandy. *Rapid Team Deployment*. Menlo Park, CA: Crisp Publications, 1995.

Pokras, Sandy. *Team Problem Solving, Revised Edition*. Menlo Park, CA: Crisp Publications, 1995.

Pokras, Sandy. *Working in Teams, Revised Edition*. Menlo Park, CA: Crisp Publications, 2002.

Simons, George. *Working Together, Third Edition*. Menlo Park, CA: Crisp Publications, 2002.

Van Daele, Carrie. *50 One-Minute Tips for Trainers*. Menlo Park, CA: Crisp Publications, 1995.

Wingfield, Barb and Janice Berry. *Retaining Your Employees*. Menlo Park, CA: Crisp Publications, 2001.

CRISP WORLDWIDE DISTRIBUTION

English language books are distributed worldwide. Major international distributors include:

ASIA/PACIFIC

Australia/New Zealand: In Learning, PO Box 1051, Springwood QLD, Brisbane, Australia 4127   Tel: 61-7-3-841-2286, Facsimile: 61-7-3-841-1580 ATTN: Messrs. Richard/Robert Gordon

Hong Kong/Mainland China: Crisp Learning Solutions, 18/F Honest Motors Building 9-11 Leighton Road, Causeway Bay, Hong Kong   Tel: 852-2915-7119, Facsimile: 852-2865-2815 ATTN: Ms. Grace Lee

Indonesia: Pt Lutan Edukasi, Citra Graha, 7th Floor, Suite 701A, Jl. Jend. Gato Subroto Kav. 35-36, Jakarta 12950 Indonesia Tel: 62-21-527-9060/527-9061 Facsimile: 62-21-527-9062 ATTN: Mr. Suwardi Luis

Japan: Phoenix Associates, Believe Mita Bldg., 8th Floor 3-43-16 Shiba, Minato-ku, Tokyo 105-0014, Japan   Tel: 81-3-5427-6231, Facsimile: 81-3-5427-6232 ATTN: Mr. Peter Owans

Malaysia, Philippines, Singapore: Epsys Pte Ltd., 540 Sims Avenue #04-01, Sims Avenue Centre, 387603, Singapore   Tel: 65-747-1964, Facsimile: 65-747-0162 ATTN: Mr. Jack Chin

CANADA

Crisp Learning Canada, 60 Briarwood Avenue, Mississauga, ON L5G 3N6 Canada Tel: 905-274-5678, Facsimile: 905-278-2801 ATTN: Mr. Steve Connolly

EUROPEAN UNION

England: Flex Learning Media, Ltd., 9-15 Hitchin Street, Baldock, Hertfordshire, SG7 6AL, England Tel: 44-1-46-289-6000, Facsimile: 44-1-46-289-2417   ATTN: Mr. David Willetts

INDIA

Multi-Media HRD, Pvt. Ltd., National House, Floor 1, 6 Tulloch Road, Appolo Bunder, Bombay, India 400-039 Tel: 91-22-204-2281, Facsimile: 91-22-283-6478 ATTN: Messrs. Ajay Aggarwal/ C.L. Aggarwal

SOUTH AMERICA

Mexico: Grupo Editorial Iberoamerica, Nebraska 199, Col. Napoles, 03810 Mexico, D.F. Tel: 525-523-0994, Facsimile: 525-543-1173   ATTN: Señor Nicholas Grepe

SOUTH AFRICA

Corporate: Learning Resources, PO Box 2806, Parklands, Johannesburg 2121, South Africa, Tel: 27-21-531-2923, Facsimile: 27-21-531-2944 ATTN: Mr. Ricky Robinson

MIDDLE EAST

Edutech Middle East, L.L.C., PO Box 52334, Dubai U.A.E. Tel: 971-4-359-1222, Facsimile: 971-4-359-6500   ATTN: Mr. A.S.F. Karim